There Is Magick All Around Us

Grimoire of Poetry

Mong-Tuyen Hetland

Made with ❤ on the BookLeaf Publishing Platform
www.bookleafpub.in
www.bookleafpub.com

Dedication

Tito, Joel, Jon, Luke

and Liv

"there is magic all around you" - Stevie Nicks

i love you MORE - i win!

Anna, Donna, Karen, Michelle, Sandy,
Stefanie and Vanessa

Unicorn Moms

and in the most unlikely of places, we
founded our coven

Acknowledgement

For some achievements to be made, it takes a village. I am deeply grateful to my family and friends who have supported me on this journey. Words cannot adequately express my appreciation for your contributions, encouragement, and presence in my life. This grimoire serves as a testament to the power of collective energy and the magick that unfolds when we come together. And though this book may fade with time, as all things quietly do, the impact of your influence will remain with me forever.

Robert Hetland. It all began with a simple, yet profound gesture – a kiss on the cheek. From that moment on, my life was changed forever. Thank you for being my unwavering support system, and allowing me to pursue my dream as a writer. Your selflessness, love, and care – including cooking countless meals when I lost track of time – have been my foundation. You embody the qualities that make a true partner, and I aspire to make you proud. I am forever grateful to have you by my side, My Love.

Joel, Jon, and Luke Hetland. My three joys and chaos! You bring an infectious energy to my life. Your antics and adventures are the perfect antidote to monotony, and I am so grateful to be along for the ride. A special thanks for shouldering responsibilities, like doing your own laundry, because I was too busy trying to get the rhyme right.

Olivia Hetland. My calm, my constant, my Polaris. I cherish the moments when people notice the resemblance between us, but I know that you are so much more than a mini-me. Like a constellation, your unique spirit, sparkle, and talents make you such a magickal wonder to admire. Thank you for cooking the pasta because I was stuck on a villanelle.

Donna Saavedra. Author, unicorn whisperer, and my dearest friend. Your motivation, insightful suggestions, and encouragement played a significant role in shaping the poems within this collection.

Your invitation to ride alongside you and your winged unicorn has made all the difference. Thank you for helping me hone in on my magick.

Sandy Bohn, Anna Bowles, Vanessa Rae Gomes, Michelle Inez Castaldi Mann, Stefanie Keefe, Karen Pfleger, and Donna Saavedra --- the Unicorn Moms. Why, of all places, the Universe decided to bring us together at "that school" remains a mystery. But, as Fate would have it, our distinct energies were woven into a rich tapestry, and our serendipitous union has given rise to a truly magickal existence. Thank you for not only the encouragement to put pen to paper, but also for being the muse for this grimoire. People should know: Not all witches are bad.

Preface

As I embarked on writing another book of poetry, I did not anticipate that it would evolve into a grimoire.

My first book, *A Book of Pressed Thorns - Poetry of Hard Things*, was a deeply personal and vulnerable account of my darkness. The experience of publishing and sharing that book was both thrilling and terrifying.
When it first became available, I felt exposed, like I had left my diary open for the world to read. But as I connected with readers who resonated with my words, I discovered that baring my soul had liberated others to share their own stories of pain and struggle.

I formed profound connections with individuals who had been touched by my work. As I focused on the magick that emerged from these relationships, I found myself drawn to a group of particularly extraordinary women. Our unique energies intertwined, and a coven was born. When the

Universe nudged me to write again, I knew I wanted to celebrate these good witches. This grimoire is a testament to their light, love, and kindness.

Since my first book was shrouded in darkness, I wanted my next one to be about the light...because there is always a light. While the rituals and spells within these pages are fictional, my family and the women who inspired them are very real. I did my best to honor the essence of their spirits. I hope you will delight in the discovery of these witches, wizards, wizardlings, and witchlets. I hope their warmth and energy reaches you, and inspires you to share your own magick.

.

So mote it be.

Awen

Her white gown shimmers pure and bright,
A beacon like the moon at night.
A White Witch with white angel wings,
Cleansing the hearts with holy things,
And sharing all the hidden Truth
For spiritual guidance to the youth.

Awen's gift, on whispered breath,
Comes from Divine's hidden depth.
Her gentle spells ignites the mind
To make sacred hearts more defined.
Magick amidst ancient birch trees,
Her prayers for you are given free.

Her protection of your heart and soul
Comes with grace; the Divine makes whole.

With silken threads she gently weaves
A tapestry among the leaves.
Each knot secured with hope and faith,
Each spell a blessing of your fate.
So next time you are in the wood
'Neath Awen's canopy of Good,
Listen for the coo of a dove:
It's the White Witch sending her love.

Spell - Divine Guidance

Upon my sacred altar, I place
White candle and crystal quartz.
With cleansing sage and frankincense
I now pray these words:

O, Higher Power of the universe,
I call for guidance, filled with endless love.
Connect me with your divine design,
And align my heart with peace from above.

I am connected, I am guided. So mote it be.

Brigid

Quickly, she bundles her lavender;
Unicorn by her side, Brigid's winged ride.
Our Lavender Witch, spell handler,
To the moon and back lunar traveler;
Her magick is spectacular.

'Tis poetry Brigid gifts, and spirits she lifts,
Healing those who are weary and worn,
Encourages faith, and make dreams reborn.

Rare moon water, dew, lavender, too:
Ancient potion from grimoire's lore,
Vitalizes each heart and soul; therefore,
Each spirit wanting less and
Never more.

Spell - The Write Spell

Sprinkle, sprinkle lavender buds,
Purple candle for the words,
Quiet space and calming scent,
Hold my pen, now my intent:

I've calmed my mind, I've freed my soul.
Calliope, words to make me whole.
Help me put my pen to page.
Writer's block exit the stage.
Thank you, Muse, for joining me.
A toast to you with lavender tea.

Beatrix

The Green Witch, her name is Beatrix,
Whose spells often sound like limericks.
They are meant to bring joy,
Her charmed stones and alloy,
To someone who needs a life fix.

Her spirit animal - her dog -
Whose unconditional pure love,
Inspires green magick:
Good luck, nothing tragic,
And joys you just can't catalog.

The Green Witch's tool is her wand,
And also a favorite cauldron.
Stir abundance and wealth
Into charms from her shelf.
You'd think these were for the beau monde.

Beatrix collects emerald and jade
For those overworked, underpaid,
So that her magick might
Let them see their own light;
And to feel blessed and unafraid.

Spell - Inner Child Out

Purple candle, patchouli oil,
Mugwort herb to burn.
Black tourmaline and fox spirit
It's whimsy that we yearn.

By trickster's wit and coyote's guile,
We unleash our inner child.
With kind heart and adventurous fire,
We dance and play, our spirit's desire.

Tag! You're it!

Enid

She must have been sent from across the stars,
Bringing with her the powers of Neptune.
Collecting stardust like fireflies in jars
To blend with magick water from Full Moon.
She is our eldest, she is our wisest,
She is peace and the spirit of Divine.
Enid is the most powerful Blue Witch
Who can heal spirits and faiths in decline.
A visit from her faithful familiars -
The rainbow butterfly and snow white swan -
Bring tidings from your conciliator:
The time has come for the next echelon.
Blue vervain and hyssop and spell for oath,
Expand consciousness and spiritual growth.

Spell - Spiritual Growth

White candle, amethyst, and sage:
I create my Sacred Space.
O, ancestors and angels,
My path, please help illuminate.

I nurture my inner soul,
And call forth Wisdom to make me whole.
With grace and love, I find my way,
To spiritual growth, each new day.

I illuminate my inner path.

Airmed

Purple Witch, Airmed, goddess of healing,
Blends chamomile and yarrow for lotion.
And she remedies all woeful feeling.

If, from a wound, you find yourself reeling,
Drink her hawthorn and foxglove potion.
Purple Witch, Airmed, goddess of healing.

Internal mold leaves much unappealing,
But mint-elder bark tea is ambrosian.
And she remedies all woeful feeling.

Broken heart is in need of concealing.
For that, a lavender cloak is woven.
Purple Witch, Airmed, goddess of healing.

Her Grove of Whispers can be revealing.
Go freely when you choose to be chosen.
And she remedies all woeful feeling.

She will lead you the way to self-healing,
With the Stone of Health for your emotion.
Purple Witch, Airmed, goddess of healing.
And she remedies all woeful feeling.

Spell - Heal to Heal

Sacred candle, pure and white,
Repel the harm with your great light.
This is a space for healing.
Sage and sweetgrass cleanse the air,
Only good vibes everywhere.
This is a space for healing.

I form this shield around myself:
Lux mea, tutela mea.
I form this shield around my health;
My light, my protection.

Suri

At twilight's hush the shadows dance,
And Suri, Red Witch, starts her chants.
Her heart aflame, a ruby fire;
Passion and power, and deepest desire.

O, Suri! Red Witch, your magick unfolds
Spells from your grimoire of secrets untold.
Give garnet strength and rose petals might;
Seal in their energy with the moon's light.

Each Tuesday, Mars' Day, let fire burn;
Red candle gifting all that is yearned.
Her altar aglow, for passion is high;
Dragon's blood and ginseng: vitality is nigh.

O, Suri! Red Witch, your magick unfolds
Spells from your grimoire of secrets untold.
Give red jasper strength and cayenne might;
Seal in their energy with the moon's light.

Each Sunday, Sun's Day, let fire burn;
Gold candle granting all that is yearned.
Her altar aglow, for healing is high;
The Healing Sunbeam Spell: the nurturing is
nigh.

O, Suri! Red Witch, your magick unfolds
Spells from your grimoire of secrets untold.
Give red ruby strength and bloodstone might;
Seal in their energy with the moon's light.

Aphrodite's love and Brigid's fire:
Woven in spell to never expire.
Carnal wisdom and secrets nocturnal,
Hushed incantations for sex eternal.

So, sunset fades, and day succumbs to night.
Sensual Suri sways in the firelight.
Her magickal dance mesmerizes you;
Because of her spell, you're seductive, too.

Spell - Unfettered

Mirror, mirror see my eyes,
Find the fears that I disguise.
Now on paper that I hold,
Candle burn to let them go.
I release all inhibitions!
Libera me, inhibere nullus!
Free me, no inhibitions!

Calliope

'Twas the night before Esbat, and all through
the land,
The witches were stirring with magick at
hand.
Calliope, the Black Witch, with her poetry
grimoire
Prepared for the ritual, with herbs and stones
as before.

The black tourmaline talismans, on her altar
did lay,

With obsidian and onyx to absorb negativity's
sway.
Patchouli and sandalwood scented the
evening air,
As Calliope invoked Hecate for magick to
share.

The raven perched outside, his silk coat
shining bright,
Watching Calliope weave her spell of
protection tonight.
The black wolf, Mystique, lay down by her
side,
As Calliope spoke ancient poetry at a
drumbeat's tide.

The waning moon cast shadows on the walls
so dark,
As Calliope danced clockwise with her
athame's spark.
The black candles, they burned like stars in
the night,
Guiding Calliope's magick with Saturn's
steady light.

Anubis and Lilith watched over her with care,
As Calliope banished fears and purified the
air.
Kali's fierce energy boldly coursed through
her veins,
Transforming doubts and worries into
empowering gains.

When the ritual ended, and the spell was cast,
Calliope smiled knowing that her poetry
would last.
The night was filled with mystery and magick
so rare,
Until next Esbat, enchantment would stay in
the air.

The raven cawed softly as Calliope blew out
the flame,
And Mystique sighed contentedly at magick's
gentle claim.
Calliope again smiled, knowing the night's
work was done,
And the poetry of the Black Witch and her
magick were one.

Spell - Protection For Poets

By the power of the poetic muse,
I give protection, pure and true.
I shield thee from doubt and criticism's sting,
And guide your words on creative wing.
With lavender's calming, peaceful sway,
And quartz's clarity, come what may.
Your heart and mind are safe and sound,
Your quill flows unhindered with inspiration now.
So mote it be, with poetic might,
You are protected each time you write.

Soleil

O, Magenta Witch!
Your magick brings children joy.
Laughter, perfect pitch.

The charoite stone
And hibiscus plant employ
Harmony at home.

Soleil, warmth and light.
Your peaceful spells soothe the soul.
Magick to delight.

Venus on Friday:
Creative expression flows.
I did it my way.

Children in wonder,
Empowered by Scorpio,
Dream loud as thunder.

Fear not to embark:
Meander like a rio
Into Soleil's heart.

Magenta candles
And dragon's blood to shield you.
Shoo away shambles.

Spirit animals:
Butterflies, hummingbirds, too.
Come! Be magickal!

Aphrodite and
Soleil, guardian angels,
With babes they will stand.

Children and villain
Will no longer entangle.
Blessed be the children.

Spell - For All the Children

I cultivate a sacred place
With this potted flower.
A little toy for girl and boy
So they can play for hours.
To represent their little world,
A tied ribbon 'round this space.
Protego totalum puellis et pueris
With my warm embrace.
Stones to shield this sacred place;
Protect all girls and boys.
Protego totalum puellis et pueris:
Protect all girls and boys.

For Mother Earth

By earth, air, fire, water, and spirit's might
We shield our home, through day and night
Terra Shield, now activated be
Guard our earth for all creatures and beings.

By ancient roots, we anchor deep
Protecting earth, in endless sleep
With winds of change, we bring forth might
Preserving air, pure and bright
Flames of transformation, burn away
Purifying fire, for a new day
Tides of emotion, flow and heal

Nourishing waters, our souls reveal
Divine light shines, guiding our way
Illuminating path, night and day
Earth's core wisdom, we now invoke
Grounding our power, with ancient cloak
Heart of love, unites us all
Binding our spell, standing tall
Sealing our shield, around this earth
Protecting all, of every birth

By earth, air, fire, water, and spirit's might
We shield our home, through day and night
Terra Shield, now activated be
Guard our earth for all creatures and beings.

Airwyn's Breath

Mother Wind, Airwyn, we pray
To protect your breath every phase.
From breeze to gale, we weave our spell,
The air is your voice; you have stories to tell.

Mother Wind, Airwyn, we summon your
might,
Orator of the skies, hear our plea tonight.
From mountaintop to valley below,
We seek to shield your breath, as it ebbs and
flows.

May Zephyr's gentle touch bring renewal and
peace,
As we weave this protective web, our
intentions release.
Let the essence of the air, your breath of life,
Flow through our veins, connecting us in
stride.
We call upon your Sylphs, the spirits of your
breeze,
To join our chant, and bring Pollution to his
knees.
From Pollution's grasp, his toxic sigh,
We shield your breath, with a love aimed
high.

Mother Wind, Airwyn, we pray
To protect your breath every phase.
From breeze to gale, we weave our spell,
The air is your voice; you have stories to tell.

Honor the Waters

By the tides of the ocean, we are gathered
here,
To honor the sea's majesty, and waters
everywhere.
Purify our intentions, and cleanse our
muddled minds,
As we connect with the ripples, and the waves
of tides.

We call upon Poseidon, Neptune, and the
Mermaids
To join our circle, and bless this ritual we've
made.

We honor the sea's power, in all its might and
fury,
We humbly seek harmony and balance in
water's purity.

Sometimes we fear the waves washing over.
Sometimes we need the shaking to bravely be
the mover.
We are grateful the waters buoy up life's ebbs
and flows,
And their depths keep our secrets no one
should know.

We thank the ocean for its bounty and might,
For the lessons it teaches about sailing
through life.
May our meager efforts be accepted with
grace,
May we remember how small we are in its
space.

If the waters accept us, our ritual is complete,
May its energy always be the soles of our feet.
We release our own energy, back into the
tides,

In hopes that our prayers remain in the
depths of time.

32

Homage to Fire

Double, double rapid boil;
Ignis burn and we are loyal.
Fillet of a dragon's blood,
Suddenly the world is good.
Pyropex, illuminate
Love and warmth you generate.
Agni, cleanse and make us whole.
Hail your glory in our soul.
Double, double Fire Drakes,
Spirited moments do you make.

Mother Moon's Blessing

By the silvery glow of your light,
We call upon your gentle might.

From New to Full, we honor your phases past,
Embracing the cycles, forever to last.

May your lunar energy, pure and bright,
Illuminate our paths, through day and night.

Let your intuitive wisdom guide our way,
As we weave this spell, come what may.

We call upon the goddesses of Mother Moon's might:
Selene, Isis, and Diana, join our delight.

From the tides of change to the stability of the shore,
We balance our energies forever more.

May our collective energy, like moonbeams bright,
Reflect our inner shine, banishing the night.

Mother Moon, your blessing, now cast and sealed,
Channeling your power, our hearts revealed.

Mother Moon's blessing, we receive,
Embracing Mother Moon's gentle reprieve.
By the light of Mother Moon, so bright,
We tap into her power, on this sacred night.

May our intentions manifest,
With Mother Moon's guidance and might,
As we release this energy,
May Mother Moon shine through the night.

Magick Pantry

My old magick pantry, it keeps my witch's herb
handy,
right next to the blue jay wings.
I burn them together, the leaf and the feather,
to create safety around my beloved things.

I heat Hestia's blood with the tongue of a dove,
and sip it from a teacup for peace,
as I reach in the cupboard for fragrant fairy's herb
and dew of the sea seasoning for meat.

Rubbing onto the meat, baking well, and then eating:
psychic powers sharpen with this magickal meal.
Dog berry and tongue, a pinch of old man season:
top on my dessert for healing a tough ordeal.

O' old magick pantry, thank you for keeping handy
the ear of goat within my reach.
Crushing that with some devil's nettle with my mortar and pestle,
I will use it for protection no evil can breach.

Come, My Little Witchlet

Come, my little witchlet, and ride upon my
broom!
We'll sweep stardust off the constellations on our
way to the Full Moon.
We'll take a swim in the Milky Way, and pirouette
along Saturn's rings,
leave wishes on the stars, and on Pluto, do all the
wintery things.

Come, my little witchlet, now let's descend to
Earth
and wander through the forest where ancient
magick came to birth.

We'll find a hidden clearing that's blessed by lunar
rays.
This is where I will teach you all our magickal
ways.
First, you'll listen for Moon's soft voice, feel her
energy ebb and flow,
Then we'll dance with our sisters as the Universe's
symphony grows.

Come, my little witchlet, let's ride the ocean
breeze!
We'll listen to the secrets that the tide whispers to
seaweeds.
We'll surf the waves with the mermaids, and sing
a dolphin song;
collect driftwood, sea glass and hag stones that
vibrate in our bones.
I'll teach you how to use them to weave a
grounding spell,
And stay centered to the sea through your
talisman shell.

Come, my little witchlet, let's return to our sacred
space:
Our home, our hearth, our altar, our favorite
blessed place.
You know your crystals, your herbs, and all the
oils on the shelf.

You're ready to rein your own broom; my
witchlet, fly free yourself!

40

Bambina's Butterfly Whisper Spell

In my garden full of hues,
here I stand, o' gentle Muse,
with a pinch of glitter, like stardust bright;
with feather and scale, both just as light.
Now, I sprinkle glitter in a circle wide;
please hear my wish I now provide:

By wings of wonder, I call to thee,
Butterfly spirits, please dance with me.
O' gentle wind, please carry my plea,
Come butterfly, whisper your stories to me.

Butterfly spirits, so mote it be.

The Three Wizardlings

With wands in hand and spirited hearts,
Three wizardlings were anxious for their training
to start.
First, the fundamentals of ancient magick long
passed:
Wield with caution the awesome power in your
grasp;
Safety and control, or disaster will come fast.

Next, in quiet chambers, you'll learn how to still
Your heart and your mind by meditation and will.
You'll focus your thoughts like a beam of light,
Calm your emotions from the darkest fears of
night.

And find inner peace that brings strength and
might.

With the elements of earth, air, fire, and sea
You'll learn that in magick, there is symmetry:
There is balance in forces, that shape and mold
When to accept the new, when to deny the old,
And to acknowledge when in fear, you are equally
as bold.

Spells and incantations you'll develop with care,
With the basics of casting, you'll add precision
and flair.
You'll learn how to channel your magick with
ease,
And direct its power with a wizard's expertise.
Your magick will manifest if you follow rules such
as these.

Above all else, Wizardlings, you must always
abide
By the ethics and morals your ancestors did
provide.
Your magick is only for the good and the right,
To maintain the balance of life's delicate light,
To wield your magick with wisdom and respectful
might.

Invocation of the Dragonfly

I've come by the water where dragonflies play,
Grasping a shell, a sprig, and opal in hand,
To invoke the dragonfly's swift command.

By these gifts, I call to thee,
Dragonfly spirits, will you dash with me?
Through realms of water, air, and light,
Bring swiftness, agility, and magick tonight.

Come, dragonfly spirits! Come guide and inspire
my wizardling heart with dragon fire.
By dragonfly speed, so mote it be.

What Witchlets and Wizardlings Are Made Of

What are witchlets made of?

They are made of stardust and snowflakes,
Ladybugs and cupcakes.
Magick and moonbeams,
Butterfly kisses and sweet dreams.
Unicorns and mermaids and rainbows above.
That is what witchlets are made of.

What are wizardlings made of?

They are made of aurora and shooting stars,
Fireflies and chocolate bars.
Wonder and might,
Sonic booms and space flight.
Dragons and tritons and starry nights above.
That is what wizardlings are made of.

A Wizard Kind of Love

O, sun-kissed witch, with chestnut eyes,
Thy beauty shines like moonbeam skies.
Thy raven tresses, like the mystery of the deep,
Invite my soul to burrow in their darkness and
sleep.
Thy lips, they curve like petals of the rose,
Inviting me to taste the sweetness that they
disclose.
Thy touch, it sparks like magick, wild electricity;
A flame that burns and never fades, a love so
fated to be.
In thy embrace I find my nest,
A haven from the world, where I lay and rest.
With thee, my love, I need not spells, no magick
beyond thine,

Together, we create a love that no starry night
outshines.
O, mystic witch, thou art my magick and my
dream,
My love, my heart, my sacred ring, my witch, my
queen.

Wizard Marriage Spell

I put the crystals in three times a day,
And then I tie the strings in a magickal way.
Red and grey beads, passion and balance, too;
I'm makin' a braid of love strong enough for me and
you.

I put the love in, and I stir it up,
And then I tie the knot so we never give up.
I'm makin' a braid of love that's real,
And I'm wearin' it close so your heart can feel.

I add some rose petals, and a little bit of flair,
And then I say some words that tell you I care

I'm makin' a promise to love and to share,
And I'm sealin' it with a kiss and a prayer.

Life can get crazy, and love can get tough,
But with this braid of love, we will weather the rough.
I'll wear it like a crown, and it'll shine so bright,
And your love will be its guiding light.

Inferno Love

In the mirror of your eyes, I see
A reflection of my own ecstasy.
A love that burns like a pyre, consuming all
Leaving only ashes and the ache of longing's thrall.
Your touch ignites a fire that sears my skin,
A flame that flickers deep within, a burning for
original sin.
I am a witch, a weaver of spells and charms,
But you, my wizard, are the one who disarms.
In your arms I am undone, a threadbare thing,
A tapestry of love unraveled, and rewoven to sing
A song of passion, of possession, of the taboo and
the divine;

A love that is both curse and blessing, intertwined
like a vine.
So, let us dance, my love, in the darkness of the
night
With every step our love shall grow a magickal,
blinding light.

Runes That Bind Spell

In the stillness,
Two runes to bind our love:
Kokoro, for heart and soul;
Ai, for love and affection.
On a stone, flat and smooth,
Kokoro above, to connect heart and mind;
Ai below, to nurture love.
I tie a thread of red, around the stone,
Binding our love with a knot.

Bina in unum cor, mens, spiritus, et amor.
Two as one in heart, mind, spirit and love.

So mote it be.

Into My Magick

O, the mystic winds, they whispered low
Of secrets kept and mysteries unknown,
A language hidden, yet I understood
The call of the craft, a heartbeat in my blood.
Have I been a witch, long before the spell?
A knowing deep within, a story to tell
Of moonlit nights and hushed incantations.
A mystic sense that guided me through life's
creations.
The sisters of the moon, they sang to my soul,
A chorus of ancient rhymes, making me whole.
The trees, the rivers, the creatures of the night
All released their magick to intertwine my light.

An urge to be a weaver of spells and charms,
A dancer in the shadows, a mystic form.
The wind in my hair, the stars up above
A symphony of magick, a labor of my love.
O, the time is right, I will take the sacred oath
To walk the path of wisdom, with heart and soul
and troth.
The mystic fires, they burn within my breast
A flame of knowledge that guide me to my best.
Now, I'm a witch with the power in my hands,
Innate weaver of magick, with ancient wisdom to
command.
And though the journey's long, and winding be
the road
I'll follow the heartbeat into my magick that is
mine alone.

My Book of Shadows

Weathered grimoire full of things:
Spells and recipes and sacred dreams,
Secrets of my lives that passed,
Wisdom meant to forever last.

Pages stained with blood and tears,
Scent of herbs lingered all these years,
Favorite pages worn and tattered
From frequent use and oils splattered.

Records of rituals done under the moon:
Dances with sisters among the ruins.
Fehu, Uruz, Thurisaz and Ansuz ---

Runes for secret messages and divination
clues.

57

O', Book of Shadows! As sacred as my heart!
A spell to protect you while we are apart:
Aperi per sanguinem meum solus!
So mote it be. My blood's sole use.